DYSTOPIA PLAYLIST

by

Jennifer Lagier

"Things fall apart; the centre cannot hold;
Mere anarchy is loosed upon the world,
The blood-dimmed tide is loosed, and everywhere
The ceremony of innocence is drowned;
The best lack all conviction, while the worst
Are full of passionate intensity."

--William Butler Yeats

Contents

A Jagged Wretchedness

Just past sunrise,
Monterey's homeless appear,
wander out of sage underbrush,
sticky monkey thickets,
rampant clumps of yellow oxalis.

Some have established camps
among eucalyptus, beneath overpasses;
others sprawl upon cold sand dunes,
protected by snarls
of washed-ashore driftwood.

On Sundays, they gather
to receive a free breakfast
served by volunteers
at Window on the Bay:
scrambled eggs, biscuits,
cups of steaming hot coffee.

With pit bulls, black garbage bags,
rusty shopping carts and cardboard signs,
they migrate from Del Monte Beach
to Highway One exits where they beg,
stationed at off-ramps among blue lupine,
wild radish, golden puddles of poppies.

A New War

"I fear that if he loses the election in 2020, there will never be a peaceful transition of power." — Michael Cohen

Congress investigates instance after instance
of presidential malfeasance—
hush money to mistresses,
foreign manipulation of U.S. elections,
treasonous acts, blatant corruption.

GOP members paint the Panderer-in-Chief's
testifying fixer as a habitual liar.
He produces cancelled checks, documentation
of hush money paid out to silence women
as evidence to back up accusations.

America splinters along
ideological fault lines.
As democracy sputters,
suffocated by ignorance, greed,
Lady Liberty weeps.

A Painting Nobody Would Ever See

My brother-in-law is dead.
His misogynist portraits
of unhappy, distorted women
who got between him and the bottle
hang like trophies
on my ex-husband's walls.

Their alcoholic father was also
an angry artist who threw away his career.
During one drunken rampage,
he sabotaged a New York opening,
slashed and smashed paintings,
trashed the gallery,
insulted his patron.

These men dedicated their lives
in a relentless dive to the bottom.
They left behind wives, lovers, children,
boxes of unread poetry,
unseen canvases,
passed on a legacy
of pain and addiction.

Alzheimer's Evening

My mother-in-law tells me
I'm a nice girl, favorite daughter.
It's her 91st birthday,
but this is one more date
she can't remember.
Her son explains what we're celebrating,
repeats it at least a dozen times
in less than an hour.

When she isn't asking
about my dead mother,
if my husband ever met
his grandparents, father,
she lapses into silence,
scowls, hangs her head.

Each week, she eats less
at Sunday dinner,
wants to go home sooner,
seems more befuddled.
Any phone call after 9 p.m.
from the memory care center
makes us jump, fear the worst.

Despite a mind erased
every few minutes
like a shaken etch-a-sketch,
her obstinate body keeps soldiering on.

Co-dependence

"In the time of the Yellow Emperor, the eldest female child would cut off parts of her body and feed her parents small pieces of her flesh until they were cured."
– Joseph Zaccardi in A Wolf Stands Alone in Water

It's insidious, training women
to embrace martyrdom,
perpetuate tradition,
maim their daughters with love.

Culture, religion serve
as potent enforcers,
indoctrination of unworthiness,
sacrifice for greater good.

Ceremonies distract and delude.
Each girl, the guest of honor,
a foot binder present at her feast
just before breaking bones.

Brain-washed, we practice
sanctioned, aspirational mutilation,
meekly feed instigating abusers
pieces of our own flesh.

Firstborn females are expected
to surrender family, abandon careers,
nurse the sick,
provide elder care.

Insatiable and ungrateful,
enabling society demands it,
consumes generation after generation,
eats our hearts last.

Crazy

I notice as a woman in the pharmacy
check-out line unloads her basket:
home pregnancy test, bag of Doritos,
midnight blue eyeliner,
toy Jedi light saber.

She flaunts chipped ebony toenails,
wears faded Levi's.
Her torn Metallica tee shirt
clings by a thread,
has seen better days.

The cashier asks about my husband,
now two years into sober recovery.
She was concerned when he stopped
buying bottles of Crown Royal daily
on his way to and from work.

A drunk, homeless man hits me up
for a dollar as I walk to my car.
We're part of the unraveling social asylum,
look for whatever erases or numbs,
doing what we can to get by.

Creaky Old Farts

"...hips and knees creak on their hinges."
— Joan Colby in *Bony Old Folks*

I observe cousins limping down the aisle
during my aunt's funeral.
One shifts painfully beside me,
unable to genuflect or kneel during
two and a half hours of memorial mass.

Looking around the parish hall,
I calculate how many have endured or require
hip and/or knee replacements,
wonder if we could negotiate
an economical group rate,
fantasize the small fortune
a good orthopedist could net.

Defective DNA predisposes us to osteoarthritis,
crumbling spines, degenerating bones,
Swiss Italians who lack cartilage.
Complaining, we creak through life,
hampered by immobility,
grinding bone upon bone.

The Dead-Before-Death Gang

They wear geezerdom
like scruffy badges of honor,
snarl at women who enter their lair,
a fetid saloon for cranky,
resentful men who have succumbed
to stale testosterone poisoning.

Looking in, I see a gang
of the living dead.
They drive away all who care,
with their pissing and moaning,
communally nurse escalating
bitterness, grudges.

They fester and stew,
obsess over ancient, exaggerated wrongs,
take privilege for granted,
imagine vindictive revenge.
The 21st Century
passes them by.

Doors Don't Open

*"The glass ceiling will go away when women help other
women break through that ceiling."*

— Indra Nooyi

Job interview questions during the 70's included:
 "Are you on birth control?"
 "Do you plan to get pregnant?"
 "Will your husband mind if you work evenings and weekends?"

Women managers were the exception,
often mimed sexist male supervisors,
perpetuated arrogant misogyny
as a means of survival.

For years, I dreamed of earning a degree
to advance my academic career.
Became a dean to improve working conditions,
campus support for at-risk students.

Instead, I was the administrator
in charge on Saturdays, nights,
dealt with tach squad, FBI,
gang banger task force.

Drive-by shootings on campus
during my watch
left me with PTSD,
killed my soul, motivation.

End of Days

"Watching White House press conferences these days is like watching psych ward orderlies try to convince their patients not to eat live pigeons whole in the exercise yard." —Daily Kos

Today Inmate Number One
declares himself "The Chosen,"
"King of Israel,"
calls the Federal Reserve Chair, "an enemy."
Earlier, he proposed purchasing Greenland.

Literate adults with critical thinking skills
grind their teeth; the economy craters.
Outraged citizens demand leadership
but get third-rate performance art,
demented reality t.v.,
Tourette syndrome twitter.

An ethically challenged lunatic
with anger management issues
holds our government hostage.
Daily, he petulantly melts down,
his tiny finger hovering
over a nuclear trigger.

Feel Like I'm Fixing to Die Flashback

"Be the first one on your block to have your boy come home in a box."
                                        — *Country Joe McDonald*

Patriotism flows, miles wide, a millimeter deep
as Cadet Bone Spurs distracts from impeachment
by assassinating General Soleimani,
blind-sides Congress, bypasses the constitution,
shocks un-consulted military leaders and allies,
puts Russia and China on the same page.

Fear of World War III escalates.
Twitterer-in-Chief vows to annihilate
Iranian cultural treasures,
spews idiotic, juvenile threats.
MAGA supporters cream their shorts
at the thought of Armageddon.

Those with both oars in the water
wonder when impotent old white men
will stop slaughtering the next generation.
Faux News network tools titillate
its addicted cult members.
They haven't figured out
it's their kids' blood
that will most likely be shed.

Friends of the NRA

Not the school children or their teachers
slaughtered in a rain of bullets
by disgruntled white men.

Not the women
assassinated during yet another
misogynistic psychotic break.

Not those with brown skin
gunned down without consequences
by gung-ho, militaristic police.

Not the victims
of domestic terrorism
at Planned Parenthood clinics.

Not survivors of Columbine,
Sandy Hook, Parkland,
Las Vegas, San Bernardino.

Friends include bought off politicians,
well-paid lobbyists, Russian money launderers,
conspiracy theorists, right -wing militia.

Miscreants roll out the red carpet,
invite Ares, Mammon and their cruel associates
to the biggest gun show in town.

Full of Trash

"It's like Barr summarized the 'Twilight' novels as 'a girl in Florida goes to third base with a wookie'." – John Oliver

We're living in the upside-down universe.
It's what you get when you cross corrupt with stupid,
add a soupcon of self-righteous smugness,
enlist the aid of Christian fundamentalist trolls.

A two year, multi-million-dollar investigation reveals
criminals saved from prosecution by incompetence
assisted by disobedience, disorganization.
Malfeasance gleefully sodomizes cancerous evil.

Cheeto-in-chief's fluffer issues a four-page fake summary,
visits various talking head "news" shows
to perform mandatory ass-kissing
in an attempt to distract rumbling voters.

Power-hungry repugs take a victory lap,
celebrate democracy's dismantlement
as brain-washed sycophants chorus
"No collusion. Total exoneration."

Ghosts of Christmases Past

I remember Christmas Eves
spent in emergency rooms
after loved ones overdosed
suffered panic attacks,
convulsed and hallucinated
from alcoholic withdrawals.

Holiday carols bring flashbacks
of Christmas Day burns,
cuts and bruises,
carving knife malfunctions
that resulted in stitches
or severed pieces of fingers.

Each year resurrects ghosts:
resentment, chest pains,
shingles, pneumonia.
All I want from Santa
is an uneventful Noel
without blood or drama.

Helter Skelter

"Helter Skelter", an apocalyptic war arising from racial tensions between blacks and whites as foretold by Charles Manson after listening to The Beatles song of the same name. —1960s - The Counterculture Flashcards

Amerikkka's manufactured race wars flare as
Grand-Wizard-in-Chief hires rabid neo-nazis
to enact xenophobic policies, stigmatize and accuse,
toss a lit match into spreading pools of gasoline.

What is the genesis of irrational hatred?
How many sound bites of poisonous propaganda
does it take to malform the brain, generate
violence against this week's scapegoat?

When a bigot claims to be "the least racist" person
despite never-ending verbal assaults on people of color,
reams of evidence documenting decades of discrimination,
his unchallenged dishonesty leaves one aghast.

The white underbelly of intolerant resentment
gives birth to virulent monsters who attack
peaceful protestors with clubs, cars and bullets,
gun down innocent children.

Martin Luther King, Jr. once said:
*"I refuse to accept the view that mankind is so tragically
bound to the starless midnight of racism and war that
the bright daybreak of peace and brotherhood
can never become a reality... I believe that
unarmed truth and unconditional love
will have the final word."*

Today, corruption reigns,
wicked deeds flourish,
falsehoods are accepted as fact.
Evil blankets our country
in unbroken darkness.

It's past time for We the People
to take corrective action,
heal a rotten society,
remove moral cancer,
replace poison with love.

Here in America

tRumpism triumphs.
Democracy is in crisis—
unemployment low,
the economy booming.

Those in power willingly trade
catastrophic species extinction,
befouled water, poisoned air,
for immediate profit.

Neo-fascist, dystopic America
drains the public treasury,
encourages violent intolerance,
control over women's bodies.

It's stupid Watergate, the end of days.
More of us feel disenfranchised, ignored.
Drug use and suicides multiply.
Rule of law has been declared obsolete.

How Democracy Dies

'The point of modern propaganda isn't only to misinform or push an agenda. It is to exhaust your critical thinking, to annihilate truth." – Garry Kasparov, chess champion

The land of the free has become
an expansive realm of the stupid.
Our reality show presidential pretender
cozies up to Russia, corrupt thugs
who help him steal an election.

Once in office, he is abetted
by gangsters and grifters,
dismantles rule of law,
shits on the constitution,
takes a twitter victory lap to delight
his illiterate, red-meat supporters.

Televised impeachment hearings
trot out Trumpanzi enablers, apologists,
improbable conspiracy theories
to deflect sworn testimony
offered up by expert witnesses.

Extortion, bribery, cover up, collusion….
As evidence mounts,
Faux News propagandists
instruct true believers
to pay no attention to truth.

What's left of democracy splinters.

I Remember Him

I see a version of my dad's smile
on my sister's face,
have inherited his stubby fingers,
wide feet and hammer toes
which strain my Birkenstock sandals.

He taught me how to shoot a .22 rifle,
then a 20-gauge shotgun,
the trick to driving a stick shift,
double clutching his yellow Bronco,
which levers and pedals to push
on the John Deere tractor.

He made me a substitute
for the son he never had,
took me pheasant hunting,
clam digging,
fishing in high Sierra streams
and the Stanislaus River.

At our local coffee house,
I bullshit with his surviving cronies,
laugh as we remember his various pranks,
can almost see him holding court at his favorite table.
He'd defy warnings from mom and doctor,
gobble forbidden maple bars,
knock back scalding black coffee with gusto.

Imagine They've Been Slighted

Another angry young white man,
seething over empowered women,
dark-skinned immigrants,
involuntary celibacy,
riled by the latest alt-right diatribe,
grabs his automatic rifle,
mows down an innocent crowd.

Moscow Mitch refuses to bring
a gun control bill
up for a vote, instead,
celebrates the death of his
2020 political opponent
by launching a twitter feed
of her imagined tombstone.

Fascist-in-Chief bloviates,
blames video games,
mental illness.
Ignores the racist screed
his mass murderer acolyte
posted to social media,
parroting familiar
campaign rally refrains.

Put the Second Amendment,
NRA, home-grown terrorists
and their legislative enablers
on notice, take action

to prevent the next slaughter
millions of fed up,
heartsick Americans demand.

Insanity

To satisfy his
illiterate, raving base,
toddler-in-chief throws a tantrum,
demands billions of taxpayer dollars
to build an expensive,
ineffective border wall
along our southern boundary.

His snit translates
into two painful weeks
of a government shutdown
enabled by spineless repugs
who continue slurping
at the public trough,
expect their own paychecks.

Federal employees
suffer without compensation,
worry about mortgages,
utility bills, feeding their families.
National Parks overflow
with uncollected feces and garbage.

The stench of incompetence
emanates from
a dysfunctional administration
installed by Russia,
headed by a doddering simpleton
illegitimately occupying the White House.

The Mango Moron Cries Wolf

"There's a good chance we'll have to declare a national emergency to build the wall."

Cheeto-in-Chief hysterically tweets
about renegade caravans.
His threats to declare
a national emergency to fund a wall
are the equivalent of crying "Squirrel!"
then watching distracted heads turn.

Craving the next drama,
he blusters, exaggerates, lies,
draws down troops from Syria,
reverses successful Obama programs,
rips up mutually beneficial agreements,
betrays allies by withdrawing from treaties.

As Rome burns to the ground,
Faux News trots out agent provocateurs
to shock, enrage, entertain.
Television talking heads
dictate policy, hijack attention,
tails wagging the dog.

Maui Buon Natale

It's three days until All Hallow's Eve.
Whaler's Village sprouts faux Christmas trees
festooned with surfboards, starfish,
purple and white orchid sprays.

Ukulele versions of traditional carols
plink from boardwalk speakers.
Humidity infuses radiating heat,
saturates wilting tourists.

White egrets blizzard downward
to jungle underbrush, soggy lawns.
Rotund doves replace partridges,
perch among plumeria limbs.

Afternoon trade winds carry gardenia perfume
between lithe palms and guest cottages.
Outrigger paddlers in poinsettia print swim trunks
dip, pull longboat oars, glide above coral reefs.

Mean

Migrant kids at the border are being denied soap, medical care, toothbrushes and blankets, but Melania is determined to better the lives of white kids throughout the country. – Red Painter, Crooks and Liars

Taking a page from the Herman Goering playbook,
racist-in-chief promotes increased immigration sweeps,
mass detentions, family separations, infants and children
stuffed into private concentration camp cages
denied medical treatment, toothbrushes, blankets.

As contractors rake in the dough,
Fox & Fiends spin reality,
parrot conspiracy theory sound bites,
rationalize crimes against humanity, assert
"You can't have a Hyatt on the border."

While sick babies cower under tinfoil covers,
cry for their mothers, sleep on concrete,
tone-deaf Melania's husband panders
to Neo-Nazi wet-dreams of sadistic power.
Her illiterate program slogan:
Be Best Ambassadors to Improve Lives of Children.

Moscow Mitch's Kangaroo Court

*Pelosi pounded Senate Republicans for wanting to forgo wit-
nesses and other evidence in trial. "Documentation, witnesses,
facts, truth, that is what they're afraid of," she said.*

*"Kangaroo court: any crudely or irregularly operated court,
especially one so controlled as to render a fair trial impossible."*
— Dictionary.com

The senate majority leader boasts,
"I'm not an impartial juror,"
vows coordination with White House lawyers
to cover up corruption, obstruction, treason.

Alt-right Faux News cultists
confuse literacy with liberalism,
rage and defame, pollute social media
with simplistic propaganda.

Republican senators stonewall,
commit to quick impeachment acquittal.
Adderall-addicted Pretender-in-chief
sniffs, rambles, unravels.

At rallies across a divided country,
frustrated constituents demand justice,
promise to bring a blue wave in November,
cleanse Washington's fouled Augean stable.

No Resistance, No Thoughts of Their Own

It's pure masochism,
watching talking bobble heads
on Sunday morning t.v. news shows,
hearing debates on whether
Individual No. 1 is racist
or just deflecting public attention
from impending impeachment.

Moscow Mitch and his lock-step clique
of corrupt GOP clones
can be counted on to parrot
the party line as dictated
by Sean Hannity and Faux News,
red meat to his ravening pack,
whatever distraction is necessary
to redirect outrage onto a new target.

This is how democracy falls.

Old Ladies

The dental hygienist is teary,
complains of an alcoholic husband,
in and out of rehab,
who always stops at a liquor store
to pick up a fifth on his way home.
He spends nights and evenings
in a drunken coma,
hallucinates and becomes abusive
when he wakes up.
She has filed for separation,
persuaded him to sign over to her
the deed to their house.
Now she wants him out
but can't quite bring herself
to pack his shit,
leave it on the sidewalk,
obtain a restraining order,
call the police,
change all the locks.

We commiserate—
I've survived the identical nightmare,
midnight trips to Emergency,
seizures and atrial fibrillation,
public embarrassment,
lies that spill from his mouth.
She and I are too old to tolerate
another hour of captive misery,
compare notes on escape strategies,

vow to protect each other's back
as we disentangle from dysfunction,
reconstruct better lives,
find healthy ways to move on.

Procrastination

Chirping smoke alarms
join the refrigerator's
change filter message
in being ignored.
Printer ink cartridges have been
depleted for over two years.
A neglected jury summons
gathers dust on the counter.

Her insurance non-renewal notice
languishes among growing piles
of correspondence, overdue bills.
Deadlines for late IRS filings
have come and gone
with no further attention.

Manana is her mantra,
a naïve belief problems
will solve themselves
without intervention.
"I'll get around to it,"
she assures me.
We both know she won't.

Purple Haze

"...lately things seem funny..." — Jimi Hendrix

I stand in my front yard, one block
from where Jimi torched his guitar,
watch squeaky bats wheel
across lavender sky.

Pink strands of drifting fog
decorate twilight's celestial purple.
Summer of love and its rock stars
are now dead and gone.

Temperatures soar; oceans rise.
Around us, glaciers melt, forests expire.
Wildfires followed by floods
deconstruct planet earth.

Not unlike the turbulent 60's,
I am surrounded by traumatic change
and wonder, is this dystopian tomorrow
or the end of our time?

Scotch and Water

In a Quonset hut officers' club
at the Cape Flattery SAC airbase,
my husband would order
a scotch and water for me to nurse
throughout the night
as he got louder, more aggressive,
until falling-down drunk.

Young airmen who
observed my unhappiness,
galloped to the rescue.
Prince Charming wannabes
led me onto the dance floor,
tried every line in the book,
to get into my pants.

On my 20th birthday,
one brought me cake,
flowers, ordered champagne,
held my hand under the table,
offered to pick up the tab
for divorce, help me
make a fresh start.

Guilt-ridden, I turned him down,
assisted my sodden mate to our car
where he pissed himself,
puked all over the upholstery.
I drove us back to the Coast Guard station,
a tiny, metal trailer
we called home.

Shooting Star

"We are all starlight, fragments of a great eruption." – Joan
Colby, from Contemplating the Owl in *Bony Old Folks*

Splinters of the mother-in-law I knew
manage an occasional cognitive jail break,
shine through the miasmic haze
of progressive dementia.

Family names are erased,
part of ongoing mental implosion
that consumes memories, her ability
to participate in conversations.

Some days she refuses to get out of bed.
Other times she'll come to our house for dinner
but has forgotten how to use a fork and knife,
eats salad and quiche with her fingers.

"You're a good daughter," she tells me
after a treat of wild blackberry ice cream.
I pack a sandwich bag with her favorite
white chocolate macadamia nut cookies.

Smooth as ICE

"Propaganda must facilitate the displacement of aggression by specifying the targets for hatred." —Joseph Goebbels

La Migra we call border patrol agents
who harass day laborers
as they queue up for jobs
outside our local Home Depot.
What was once a banal nature cliché
is now a potential death sentence.
Immigration officials carry out
cruel federal policy like good little Nazis.

Enraged, I carry a picket sign,
march and chant with
ACLU and MALDEF members,
parade along wire cages
where deportees are held
at the edge of Salinas.

School attendance drops.
Children are afraid of being separated
from mothers and fathers,
the only culture and community
they've ever known.

Hate-mongers scapegoat, demonize,
use faux news to rouse
their raving base, build support for
crimes against humanity,
deny the label of racist.

Somewhere

He swears he's been two years sober
as she watches him sweat, puke, convulse
on emergency room gurney.
Nurses administer haldol, ativan, verced
which do nothing to ease
his violent withdrawals.
He thrashes, cries out,
begs someone to kill him.
At the moment, she is
more than willing to comply,
if provided a weapon.

Somewhere, happy couples
sip champagne,
organize exotic trips,
plan for their future.
This blueprint will
never be theirs.
"One day at a time,"
she reminds herself.
The doctor injects an antidote.
Her mate escapes into coma.

Sympathy for the Devil

"Please allow me to introduce myself
I'm a man of wealth and taste
I've been around for a long, long year
Stole many a man's soul and faith" – The Rolling Stones

I tire of signing ineffective online petitions,
conducting intensive online research,
exercising critical thinking skills
to determine truth for myself.

Rolling around in cyber mud
with propaganda-programmed trolls
leaves me frustrated, depressed.
They spout jingoistic sound bites,
inflammatory memes untethered from fact.

Infotainment hosts replace hard news
with hate bombs, generate faux outrage,
attract emotional viewers who vent and lament
in superficial response.

Advertisers benefit, sell sham participation
followed by impulse purchases, vicious behavior,
an accumulation of bullshit,
all useless crap.

The Last of Your Mind

"Trump Tilts At Windmills At G7 While Ducking Climate Change Question"—Crooks and Liars headline

Cognitively impaired moron in chief suggests
using nuclear bombs to neutralize hurricanes
heading toward the U.S., accuses media
of "Fake News" when they report this.

Hourly, new scandals erupt,
Russian oligarchs co-signing
his money laundering loans,
brain farts transform to policy through twitter.

Funds diverted from emergency services,
sensitive public lands sold to oil men,
trade wars destabilize the economy,
send stocks into free fall.

Opening the morning paper
sends the average citizen
into toxic shock.
We all want an electoral redo.

Thoughts and Prayers

*"'Really angry' gunman who killed 3 at Gilroy Garlic Festival
cut fence, shot randomly for less than a minute." – USA Today*

While I attend a Monterey poetry reading where
two Latino poets promote love and unity,
one more furious white man cuts through a fence,
with his automatic rifle, shoots down
fifteen festival attendees, killing three,
including a six-year-old boy,
thirteen-year old girl.

When will we, as a nation,
discontinue spewing useless aphorisms,
no longer facilitate poison
seeping into hearts and minds,
bind wounds, staunch hatred,
reject division, halt wanton bleeding?

When do we quit mouthing platitudes,
lance festering resentments,
drain away sickness, cauterize anger,
make America safe and sane again,
put rational adults
in charge of our healing?

Please, no more thoughts and prayers,
just moral leadership, meaningful action.

To the End

*"Masturbating in the factory of facts...." – Adrienne Rich in
The Phenomenology of Anger*

We watch Congress play Whack a Mole
as whistleblowers reveal layers of criminality,
connect the dots between treasonous acts
and delivery of bribes, favors, payoffs.

Pretender in Chief green lights Kurdish genocide,
high stakes distraction to give Putin
exactly what he wants—kills two birds
with one cruel, petulant tantrum.

Mainstream media misses the truth,
spews whatever talking points
Watergate wannabes in the White House
have carelessly provided.

We salivate for justice, restoration of normalcy.
Blackmailed/brainwashed sycophants ignore
overwhelming evidence of unlawfulness,
incompetence, corruption, unfitness.

Waiting to Die

I never thought I'd live this long
she complains daily,
spends more and more hours
curled up in bed.

Nightly, we worry where to find
money to pay her rent,
provide round the clock nursing,
the last of her funds about to run out.

I wish it would end
she laments, echoing my mother
who endured ten months of agony,
dying of cancer by excruciating degrees.

Drug companies, nursing homes, chemotherapy clinics
profit from prolonged misery,
have a vested interest in delaying
inescapable death.

Walking the Plank

*"To be forced to accept the consequences of something. The phrase refers to the idea of pirates forcing their prisoners to **walk off a plank** on a ship and ultimately drown in the ocean."*
– The Free Dictionary

To preserve vanishing Monterey Bay dunes,
board walks protect fragile sand.

Rough wood spares native plants, coastal sage
from relentless erosion caused by rising ocean.

Our abused planet burns. Glaciers melt.
Over a million species are at risk of extinction.

We refuse to give up our unhealthy addictions,
sow toxicity into air, earth and water.

Watch us walk the plank,
drown in destruction of our own doing.

Warding Off the Weariness

We pass each other every morning
as I walk the dogs, both of us
determined to keep moving,
pushing ourselves forward
despite arthritis, scoliosis,
contortions inflicted by age.

Around us, youthful joggers,
spandexed bicyclists streak by,
their low body mass indexes,
six pack abs, muscular thighs
remind us of what we once flaunted,
now gone to seed.

Sunrise brings new infirmities,
frozen joints, forgetfulness.
As the young and beautiful
leave us in the dust,
we commiserate over relentless decline,
vent futile complaints.

What They Have Given Us

Conspiracy theories.
Gutted environmental protections.
Refusal to consider gun control
despite constituent pleas,
weekly mass murders.

Tariffs and trade wars.
Corruption, cruelty,
xenophobia, sex crimes.
Turning a blind eye
to more Russian hacking.

Nepotism, malfeasance.
Women and immigrant bashing.
Rising white supremacy.
Cavalier hate speech
dividing the nation.

Pay-offs to corporate funders.
Dismantling the social safety net.
Transforming ICE and the DOJ
into a third-world junta
composed of goon squads.

Appointment of the least competent
and most sadistic to positions of power.
Incentive for revolution.
Justification for impeachment,
indictments, violent upheaval.

Without Heart or Thought

You wish you could materialize
his frequently misplaced wallet,
keyring, cell phone,
place missing items
into his empty palm,
suck back your sarcastic remarks.

A cold coffee pot
sulks upon the stone counter.
Clock hands click
past any point of return.
Dogs cower, vanish
beneath kitchen chairs.

"You just had to say it,"
he snarls, flings borrowed car keys
onto dining room table,
a red-faced, six foot two
scowling toddler
throwing a tantrum.

You Can See

It's a familiar story:
young woman,
high school drop-out,
pregnant by 18,
living with abusive boyfriend
a paroled felon with
zero chance of employment.

Standing on the sidelines
you can see coming train wreck,
stifle the urge to intercede,
force yourself to permit her
the freedom to fuck up, fail,
figure out how to repair
her own fatal mistakes.

Acknowledgements

"A New War," *Winedrunk Sidewalk*

"Co-dependence," *Winedrunk Sidewalk*

"Crazy," *I Am Not a Silent Poet*

"Dead-before-death Gang," *Winedrunk Sidewalk*

"Feel Like I'm Fixin' to Die Flashback," *Winedrunk Sidewalk*

"Friends of the NRA," & "Doors Don't Open," *Harbinger Asylum*

"End of Days," *Winedrunk Sidewalk*

"Mean" & "Full of Trash," *I Am Not a Silent Poet*

"Ghosts of Christmases Past," *Winedrunk Sidewalk*

"The Mango Moron Cries Wolf," *Winedrunk Sidewalk*

"No Resistance, No Thoughts of Their Own," *Winedrunk Sidewalk*

"Old Ladies," *Rockford Review*

"Purple Haze," *Rockford Review*

"Scotch and Water," *Nerve Cowboy*

"Smooth As ICE," *I Am Not a Silent Poet*

"Sympathy for the Devil," *Winedrunk Sidewalk*

"The Last of Your Mind," *Winedrunk Sidewalk*

"What They Have Given Us" & "Thoughts and Prayers," *I Am Not a Silent Poet*

"To the End," *Winedrunk Sidewalk*

"Without Heart or Thought," *Good Works Review*